VIOLIN

101 CLASSICAL THEMES

Available for
FLUTE, CLARINET, ALTO SAX, TENOR SAX, TRUMPET,
HORN, TROMBONE, VIOLIN, VIOLA, CELLO

ISBN 978-1-4950-5631-4

HAL•LEONARD®
CORPORATION

7777 W. BLUEMOUND RD. P.O. BOX 13819 MILWAUKEE, WI 53213

In Australia Contact:
Hal Leonard Australia Pty. Ltd.
4 Lentara Court
Cheltenham, Victoria, 3192 Australia
Email: ausadmin@halleonard.com.au

CONTENTS

1812 OVERTURE
(Theme)

VIOLIN

PYOTR IL'YICH TCHAIKOVSKY

AIR
from WATER MUSIC

GEORGE FRIDERIC HANDEL

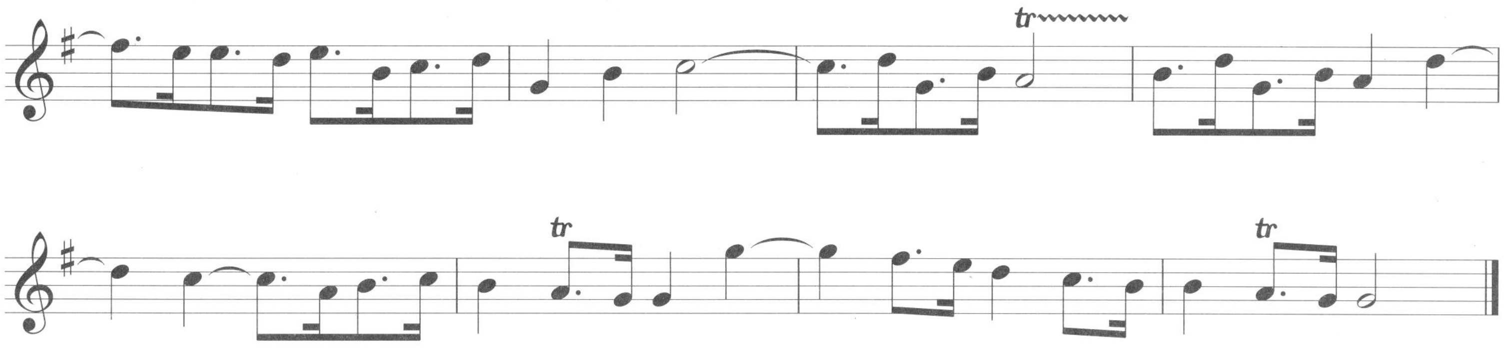

AIR ON THE G STRING

from ORCHESTRAL SUITE NO. 3

JOHANN SEBASTIAN BACH

ARIOSO

from CANTATA 156

VIOLIN

JOHANN SEBASTIAN BACH

AVE MARIA

based on “Prelude in C Major” by Johann Sebastian Bach

VIOLIN

CHARLES GOUNOD

ANDANTE CANTABILE
from STRING QUARTET NO. 1

VIOLIN

PYOTR IL'YICH TCHAIKOVSKY

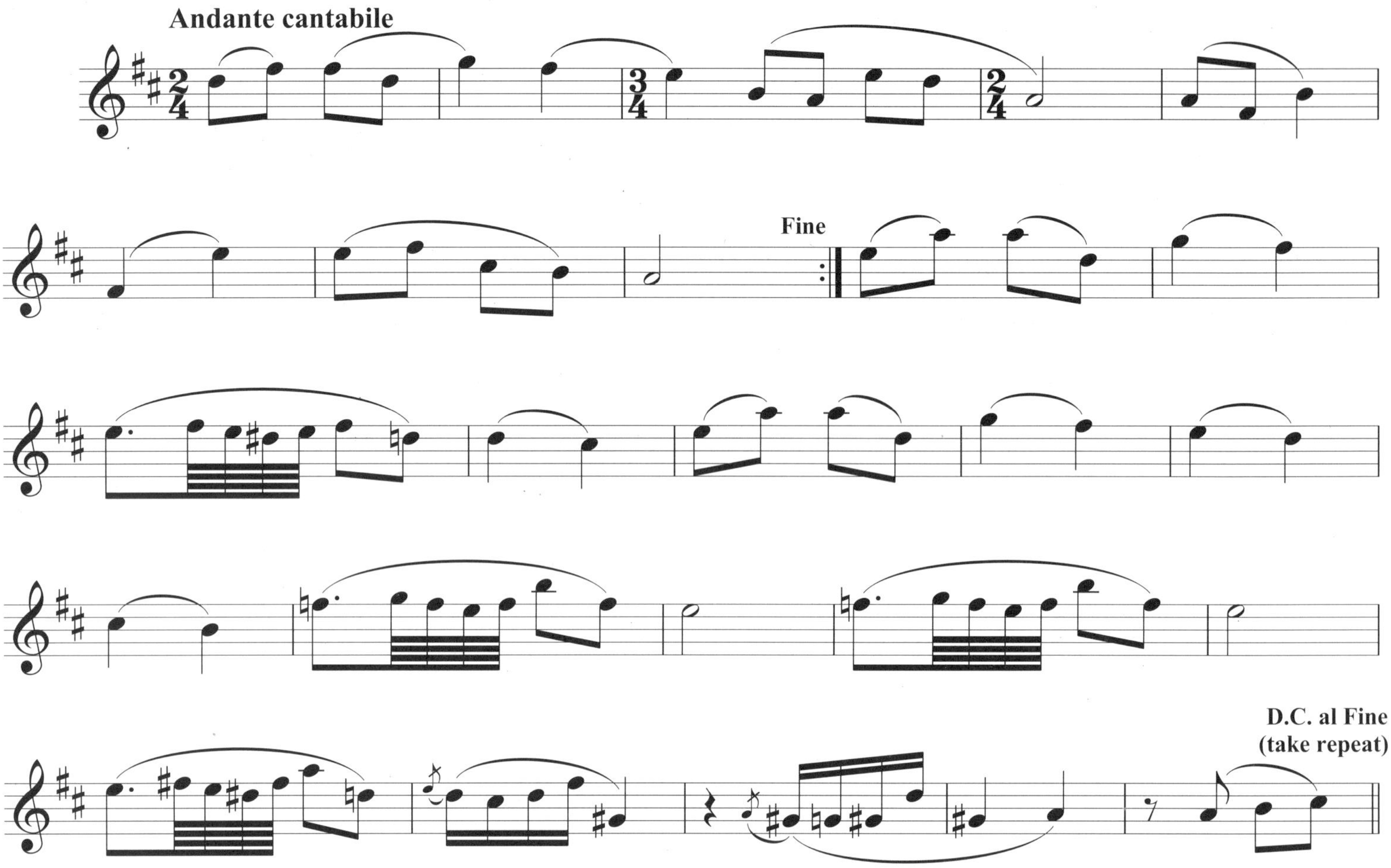

AVE MARIA

FRANZ SCHUBERT

BIST DU BEI MIR

GOTTFRIED HEINRICH STÖZEL
(previously attributed to J.S. Bach)

AVE VERUM CORPUS

VIOLIN

WOLFGANG AMADEUS MOZART

BADINERIE

from ORCHESTRAL SUITE NO. 2

VIOLIN

JOHANN SEBASTIAN BACH

BARCAROLLE

from THE TALES OF HOFFMANN

VIOLIN

JACQUES OFFENBACH

BLUE DANUBE WALTZ

VIOLIN

JOHANN STRAUSS, JR.

BOURRÉE IN E MINOR

from LUTE SUITE IN E MINOR

VIOLIN

JOHANN SEBASTIAN BACH

BRANDENBURG CONCERTO NO. 3

(First Movement Theme)

JOHANN SEBASTIAN BACH

BRANDENBURG CONCERTO NO. 5

(First Movement Theme)

JOHANN SEBASTIAN BACH

Moderately

BRIDAL CHORUS

from LOHENGRIN

VIOLIN

RICHARD WAGNER

CLAIR DE LUNE
from SUITE BERGAMASQUE

VIOLIN

CLAUDE DEBUSSY

CAN CAN

from ORPHEUS IN THE UNDERWORLD

VIOLIN

JACQUES OFFENBACH

Allegretto moderato

CANON IN D

JOHANN PACHELBEL

Adagio

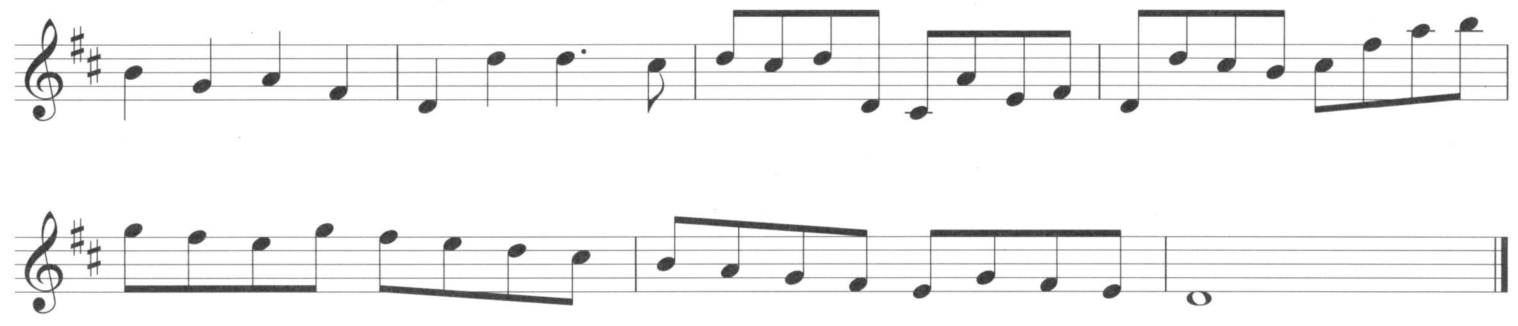

CARO MIO BEN

TOMMASO GIORDANI

DANCE OF THE HOURS

from LA GIOCONDA

VIOLIN

AMILCARE PONCHIELLI

DANCE OF THE REED-FLUTES

from THE NUTCRACKER

VIOLIN

PYOTR IL'YICH TCHAIKOVSKY

DANCE OF THE SPIRITS

from ORFEO ED EURIDICE

VIOLIN

CHRISTOPH WILLIBALD VON GLUCK

DANCE OF THE SUGAR PLUM FAIRY

from THE NUTCRACKER

PYOTR IL'YICH TCHAIKOVSKY

EINE KLEINE NACHTMUSIK

(First Movement Theme)

WOLFGANG AMADEUS MOZART

EVENING PRAYER
from HANSEL AND GRETEL

VIOLIN

ENGELBERT HUMPERDINCK

Moderately

THE FLIGHT OF THE BUMBLEBEE

NICOLAI RIMSKY-KORSAKOV

Vivace

EINE KLEINE NACHTMUSIK

(Second Movement Theme: "Romanze")

VIOLIN

WOLFGANG AMADEUS MOZART

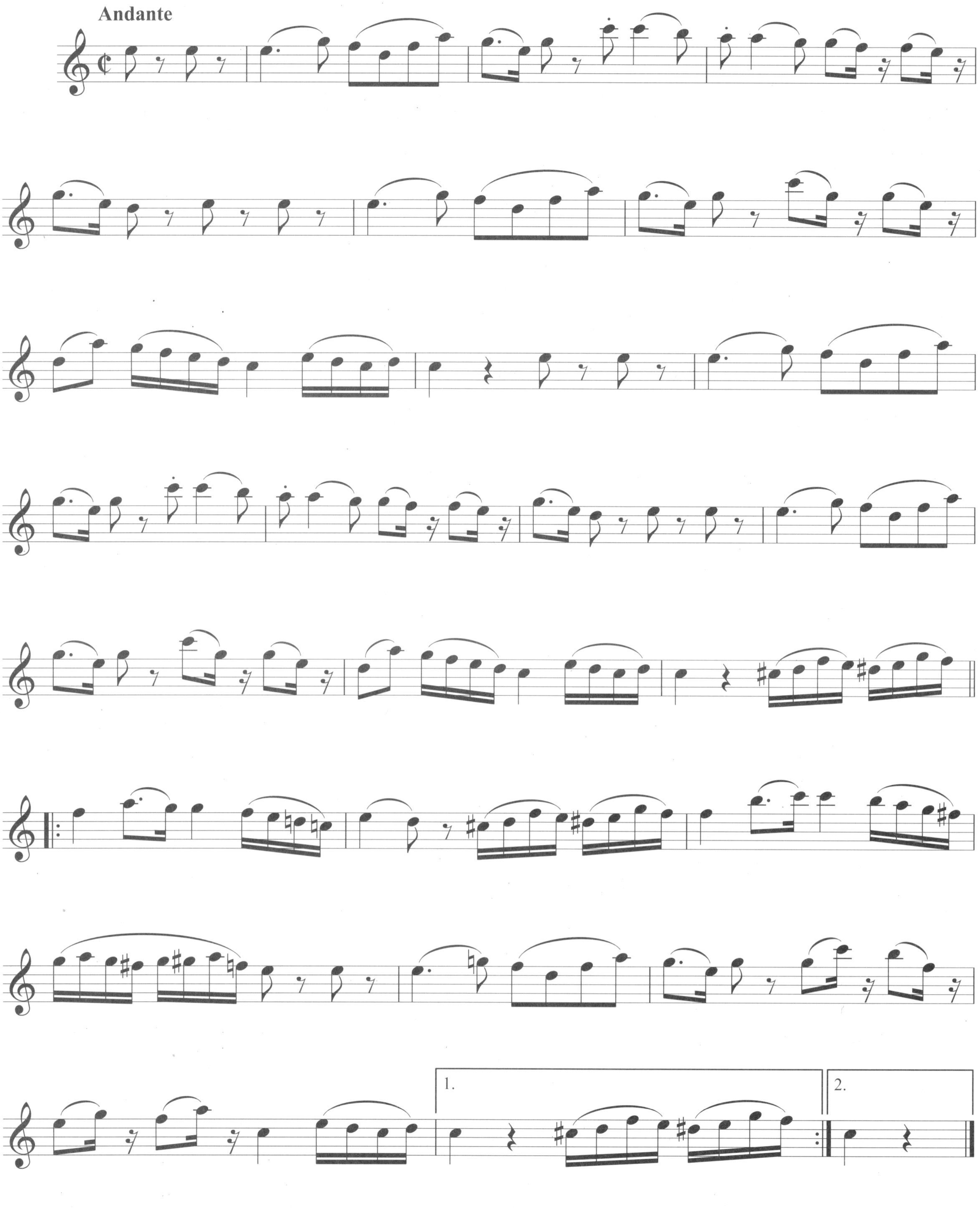

FLOWER DUET
from LAKMÉ

VIOLIN

LÉO DELIBES

Andantino con moto

FUNERAL MARCH

(Marche funèbre)

from PIANO SONATA NO. 2

VIOLIN

FRÉDÉRIC CHOPIN

FUNERAL MARCH OF A MARIONETTE

VIOLIN

CHARLES GOUNOD

FÜR ELISE

(Bagatelle No. 25)

VIOLIN

LUDWIG VAN BEETHOVEN

THE GREAT GATE OF KIEV

from PICTURES AT AN EXHIBITION

MODEST MUSSORGSKY

GYMNOPÉDIE NO. 1

ERIC SATIE

HABANERA
from CARMEN

VIOLIN

GEORGES BIZET

Allegro quasi andantino

THE HAPPY FARMER

from ALBUM FOR THE YOUNG

VIOLIN

ROBERT SCHUMANN

Brightly, cheerfully

THE HARMONIOUS BLACKSMITH

from HARPSICHORD SUITE NO. 5

GEORGE FRIDERIC HANDEL

Andante

HORNPIPE

from WATER MUSIC

VIOLIN

GEORGE FRIDERIC HANDEL

HUNGARIAN DANCE NO. 5

VIOLIN

JOHANNES BRAHMS

HALLELUJAH CHORUS

from MESSIAH

VIOLIN

GEORGE FRIDERIC HANDEL

INTERMEZZO

from CAVALLERIA RUSTICANA

PIETRO MASCAGNI

JERUSALEM

HUBERT PARRY

Moderately

IN THE HALL OF THE MOUNTAIN KING

from PEER GYNT

VIOLIN

EDVARD GRIEG

JESU, JOY OF MAN'S DESIRING

from CANTATA 147

VIOLIN

JOHANN SEBASTIAN BACH

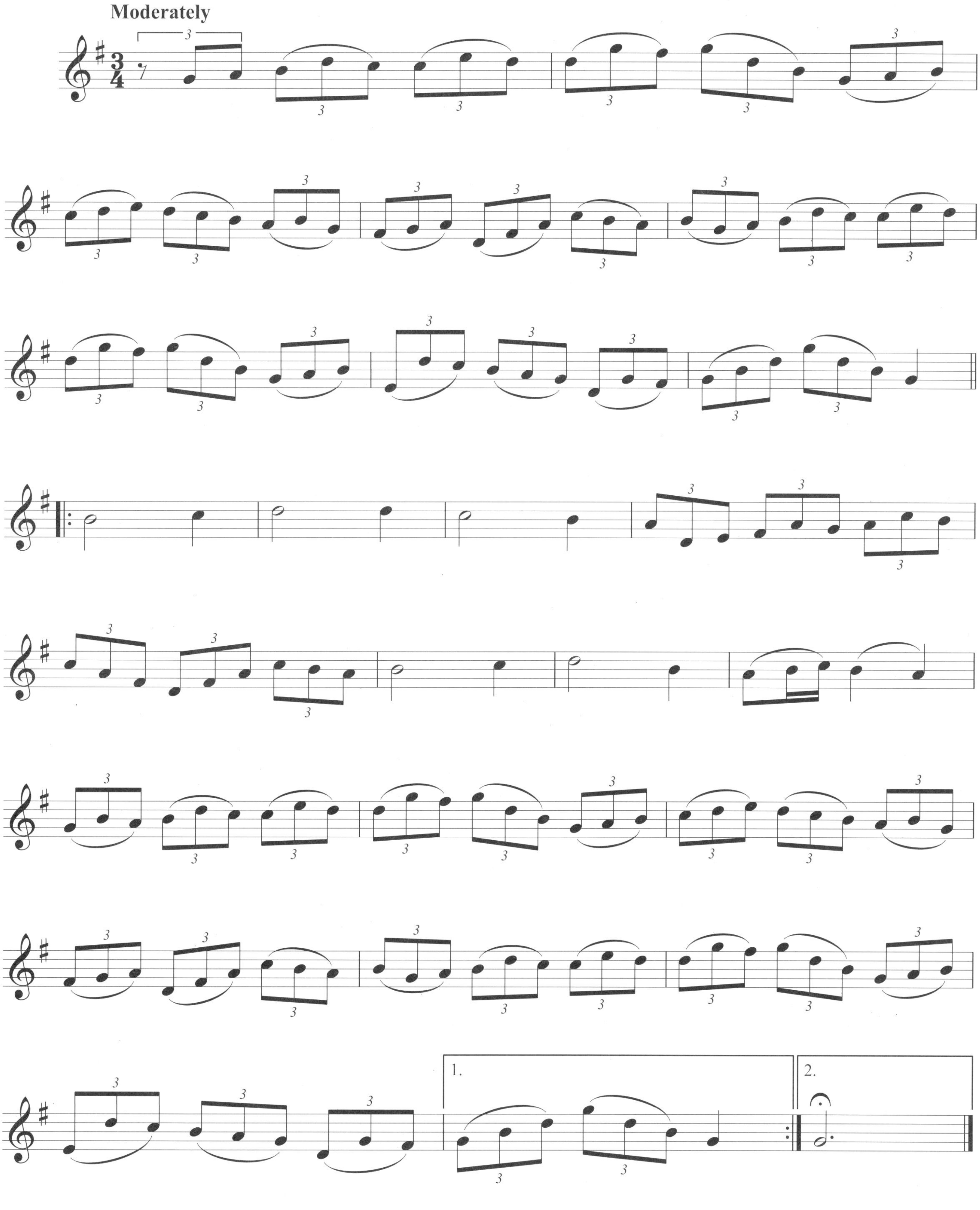

LARGO
from XERXES

VIOLIN

GEORGE FRIDERIC HANDEL

Larghetto

LAUDATE DOMINUM

from VESPERAE SOLENNES DE CONFESSORE

VIOLIN

WOLFGANG AMADEUS MOZART

LULLABY

(Wiegenlied)

VIOLIN

JOHANNES BRAHMS

Moderately, tenderly

LIEBESTRAUM

FRANZ LISZT

Poco allegro

MELODY IN F

ANTON RUBINSTEIN

MARCH
from THE NUTCRACKER

VIOLIN

PYOTR IL'YICH TCHAIKOVSKY

MARCHE SLAVE

VIOLIN

PYOTR IL'YICH TCHAIKOVSKY

MINUET
from STRING QUINTET NO. 5

VIOLIN

LUIGI BOCCHERINI

OVERTURE
from THE NUTCRACKER

VIOLIN

PYOTR IL'YICH TCHAIKOVSKY

MORNING

from PEER GYNT

VIOLIN

EDVARD GRIEG

MINUET IN G

from ANNA MAGDALENA NOTEBOOK

JOHANN SEBASTIAN BACH

MINUET IN G

VIOLIN

LUDWIG VAN BEETHOVEN

Moderately

ODE TO JOY

from SYMPHONY NO. 9

LUDWIG VAN BEETHOVEN

Allegro

PANIS ANGELICUS

CESAR FRANCK

PIANO SONATA NO. 8: "PATHÉTIQUE"

(Second Movement Theme)

VIOLIN

LUDWIG VAN BEETHOVEN

PIANO CONCERTO IN A MINOR

(First Movement Theme)

EDVARD GRIEG

PIANO CONCERTO NO. 21
(Second Movement Theme)

WOLFGANG AMADEUS MOZART

PAVANE

VIOLIN

GABRIEL FAURÉ

PIE JESU
from REQUIEM

VIOLIN

GABRIEL FAURÉ

PIANO SONATA IN C MAJOR

(First Movement Theme)

VIOLIN

WOLFGANG AMADEUS MOZART

PRELUDE IN A MAJOR, OP. 28, NO. 7

FRÉDÉRIC CHOPIN

POLOVETZIAN DANCE

from PRINCE IGOR

VIOLIN

ALEXANDER BORODIN

PRELUDE IN C MINOR, OP. 28, NO. 20

VIOLIN

FRÉDÉRIC CHOPIN

SINFONIA

from CHRISTMAS ORATORIO

JOHANN SEBASTIAN BACH

ROMEO AND JULIET

(Love Theme)

VIOLIN

PYOTR IL'YICH TCHAIKOVSKY

POMP AND CIRCUMSTANCE

VIOLIN

EDWARD ELGAR

Largamente

RONDEAU

JEAN-JOSEPH MOURET

Moderately

RONDO ALLA TURCA

from PIANO SONATA NO. 11

WOLFGANG AMADEUS MOZART

SHEEP MAY SAFELY GRAZE

from CANTATA 208

VIOLIN

JOHANN SEBASTIAN BACH

Moderately

THE SORCERER'S APPRENTICE

(Theme)

PAUL DUKAS

March tempo, in 1

SPRING

from THE FOUR SEASONS
(First Movement Theme)

ANTONIO VIVALDI

SICILIANO

from FLUTE SONATA NO. 2

VIOLIN

JOHANN SEBASTIAN BACH

SKATERS WALTZ

VIOLIN

ÉMILE WALDTEUFEL

SLEEPERS, AWAKE

from CANTATA 140

VIOLIN

JOHANN SEBASTIAN BACH

SPINNING SONG

VIOLIN

ALBERT ELLMENREICH

SWAN LAKE

(Theme)

VIOLIN

PYOTR IL'YICH TCHAIKOVSKY

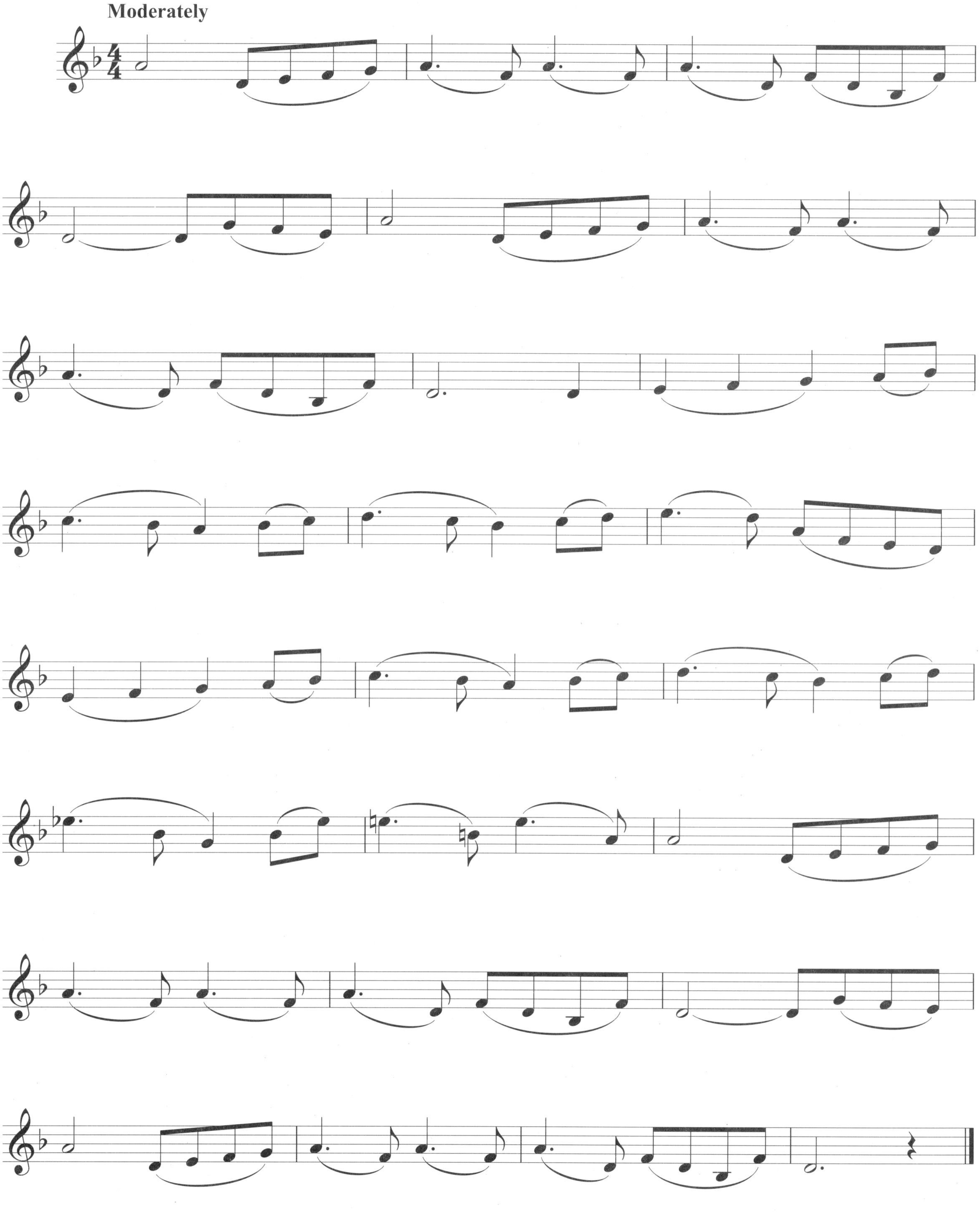

SYMPHONY NO. 5
(First Movement Theme)

VIOLIN

LUDWIG VAN BEETHOVEN

SYMPHONY NO. 1

(Fourth Movement Theme)

VIOLIN

JOHANNES BRAHMS

Allegro non troppo

SYMPHONY NO. 7

(Second Movement Theme)

LUDWIG VAN BEETHOVEN

Allegretto

SYMPHONY NO. 9

"From the New World"
(Second Movement Theme)

ANTONÍN DVOŘÁK

SYMPHONY NO. 40

(First Movement Theme)

VIOLIN

WOLFGANG AMADEUS MOZART

SYMPHONY NO. 40
(Third Movement Theme)

VIOLIN

WOLFGANG AMADEUS MOZART

TALES FROM THE VIENNA WOODS

VIOLIN

JOHANN STRAUSS, JR.

Waltz tempo

TO A WILD ROSE

from WOODLAND SKETCHES

VIOLIN

EDWARD MACDOWELL

SURPRISE SYMPHONY

(Symphony No. 94, Second Movement Theme)

VIOLIN

FRANZ JOSEPH HAYDN

Andante

TRÄUMERAI

from SCENES FROM CHILDHOOD

ROBERT SCHUMANN

Moderately

TRUMPET TUNE

HENRY PURCELL

Moderately

TRUMPET VOLUNTARY

(Prince of Denmark's March)

VIOLIN

JEREMIAH CLARKE

WILLIAM TELL OVERTURE

(Theme)

VIOLIN

GIOACHINO ROSSINI

UNFINISHED SYMPHONY

(Symphony No. 8)
(First Movement Theme)

VIOLIN

FRANZ SCHUBERT

Allegro moderato

WALTZ OF THE FLOWERS

from THE NUTCRACKER

PYOTR IL'YICH TCHAIKOVSKY

Waltz tempo

WALTZ IN C-SHARP MINOR, OP. 64, NO. 2

VIOLIN

FRÉDÉRIC CHOPIN

TOREADOR SONG

from CARMEN

VIOLIN

GEORGES BIZET

WEDDING MARCH

from A MIDSUMMER NIGHT'S DREAM

FELIX MENDELSSOHN

WHERE'ER YOU WALK

from SEMELE

VIOLIN

GEORGE FRIDERIC HANDEL

THE WILD HORSEMAN

from ALBUM FOR THE YOUNG

ROBERT SCHUMANN

WINTER

from THE FOUR SEASONS
(Second Movement Theme)

ANTONIO VIVALDI

101 SONGS

BIG COLLECTIONS OF FAVORITE SONGS
ARRANGED FOR SOLO INSTRUMENTALISTS.

101 BROADWAY SONGS

00154199 Flute..............$15.99
00154200 Clarinet.......$15.99
00154201 Alto Sax........$15.99
00154202 Tenor Sax....$16.99
00154203 Trumpet.......$15.99
00154204 Horn............$15.99
00154205 Trombone...$15.99
00154206 Violin............$15.99
00154207 Viola..$15.99
00154208 Cello..$15.99

101 DISNEY SONGS

00244104 Flute............$17.99
00244106 Clarinet.......$17.99
00244107 Alto Sax.......$17.99
00244108 Tenor Sax...$17.99
00244109 Trumpet.......$17.99
00244112 Horn..............$17.99
00244120 Trombone...$17.99
00244121 Violin.............$17.99
00244125 Viola..$17.99
00244126 Cello..$17.99

101 MOVIE HITS

00158087 Flute............$15.9
00158088 Clarinet.......$15.9
00158089 Alto Sax......$15.9
00158090 Tenor Sax...$15.9
00158091 Trumpet........$15.9
00158092 Horn.............$15.9
00158093 Trombone...$15.9
00158094 Violin............$15.9
00158095 Viola..$15.9
00158096 Cello..$15.9

101 CHRISTMAS SONGS

00278637 Flute............$15.99
00278638 Clarinet.......$15.99
00278639 Alto Sax......$15.99
00278640 Tenor Sax..$15.99
00278641 Trumpet........$15.99
00278642 Horn............$14.99
00278643 Trombone...$15.99
00278644 Violin...........$15.99
00278645 Viola..$15.99
00278646 Cello..$15.99

101 HIT SONGS

00194561 Flute..............$17.99
00197182 Clarinet.........$17.99
00197183 Alto Sax........$17.99
00197184 Tenor Sax.....$17.99
00197185 Trumpet.........$17.99
00197186 Horn..............$17.99
00197187 Trombone.....$17.99
00197188 Violin.............$17.99
00197189 Viola..$17.99
00197190 Cello..$17.99

101 POPULAR SONGS

00224722 Flute............$17.9
00224723 Clarinet.......$17.9
00224724 Alto Sax......$17.9
00224725 Tenor Sax...$17.9
00224726 Trumpet.......$17.9
00224727 Horn.............$17.9
00224728 Trombone...$17.9
00224729 Violin...........$17.9
00224730 Viola..$17.9
00224731 Cello..$17.9

101 CLASSICAL THEMES

00155315 Flute..............$15.99
00155317 Clarinet.........$15.99
00155318 Alto Sax........$15.99
00155319 Tenor Sax.....$15.99
00155320 Trumpet.......$15.99
00155321 Horn..............$15.99
00155322 Trombone....$15.99
00155323 Violin............$15.99
00155324 Viola..$15.99
00155325 Cello..$15.99

101 JAZZ SONGS

00146363 Flute.............$15.99
00146364 Clarinet........$15.99
00146366 Alto Sax.......$15.99
00146367 Tenor Sax....$15.99
00146368 Trumpet.......$15.99
00146369 Horn.............$14.99
00146370 Trombone...$15.99
00146371 Violin.............$15.99
00146372 Viola..$15.99
00146373 Cello..$15.99

101 MOST BEAUTIFUL SONG

00291023 Flute.............$16.9
00291041 Clarinet.........$16.9
00291042 Alto Sax........$17.9
00291043 Tenor Sax.....$17.9
00291044 Trumpet.......$16.9
00291045 Horn.............$16.9
00291046 Trombone...$16.9
00291047 Violin............$16.9
00291048 Viola..$16.9
00291049 Cello..$17.9

See complete song lists and sample pages at www.halleonard.com

HAL•LEONARD®
www.halleonard.com

Prices, contents and availability subject to change without notice.

HAL•LEONARD INSTRUMENTAL PLAY-ALONG

Your favorite songs are arranged just for solo instrumentalists with this outstanding series. Each book includes great full-accompaniment play-along audio so you can sound just like a pro!

Check out **halleonard.com** for songlists and more titles!

12 Pop Hits
12 songs
00261790 Flute
00261791 Clarinet
00261792 Alto Sax
00261793 Tenor Sax
00261794 Trumpet
00261795 Horn
00261796 Trombone
00261797 Violin
00261798 Viola
00261799 Cello

The Very Best of Bach
15 selections
00225371 Flute
00225372 Clarinet
00225373 Alto Sax
00225374 Tenor Sax
00225375 Trumpet
00225376 Horn
00225377 Trombone
00225378 Violin
00225379 Viola
00225380 Cello

The Beatles
15 songs
00225330 Flute
00225331 Clarinet
00225332 Alto Sax
00225333 Tenor Sax
00225334 Trumpet
00225335 Horn
00225336 Trombone
00225337 Violin
00225338 Viola
00225339 Cello

Chart Hits
12 songs
00146207 Flute
00146208 Clarinet
00146209 Alto Sax
00146210 Tenor Sax
00146216 Cello
00146212 Horn
00146213 Trombone
00146214 Violin
00146211 Trumpet

Christmas Songs
12 songs
00146855 Flute
00146858 Clarinet
00146859 Alto Sax
00146860 Tenor Sax
00146862 Trumpet
00146863 Horn
00146864 Trombone
00146866 Violin
00146867 Viola
00146868 Cello

Contemporary Broadway
15 songs
00298704 Flute
00298705 Clarinet
00298706 Alto Sax
00298707 Tenor Sax
00298708 Trumpet
00298709 Horn
00298710 Trombone
00298711 Violin
00298712 Viola
00298713 Cello

Disney Movie Hits
12 songs
00841420 Flute
00841687 Oboe
00841421 Clarinet
00841422 Alto Sax
00841686 Tenor Sax
00841423 Trumpet
00841424 Horn
00841425 Trombone
00841426 Violin
00841427 Viola
00841428 Cello

Prices, contents, and availability subject to change without notice.

Disney Solos
12 songs
00841404 Flute
00841406 Alto Sax
00841407 Horn
00841411 Viola
00841506 Oboe
00841409 Trumpet
00841410 Violin
00841412 Cello
00841405 Clarinet/Tenor Sax
00841408 Trombone/Baritone
00841553 Mallet Percussion

Dixieland Favorites
15 songs
00268756 Flute
00268757 Clarinet
00268758 Alto Sax
0068759 Trumpet
00268760 Trombone

Billie Eilish
9 songs
00345648 Flute
00345649 Clarinet
00345650 Alto Sax
00345651 Tenor Sax
00345652 Trumpet
00345653 Horn
00345654 Trombone
00345655 Violin
00345656 Viola
00345657 Cello

Favorite Movie Themes
13 songs
00841166 Flute
00841167 Clarinet
00841169 Alto Sax
00841168 Trumpet
00841170 Trombone
00841296 Violin

Gospel Hymns
15 songs
00194648 Flute
00194649 Clarinet
00194650 Alto Sax
00194651 Tenor Sax
00194652 Trumpet
00194654 Trombone
00194655 Violin
00194656 Viola
00194657 Cello

Great Classical Themes
15 songs
00292727 Flute
00292728 Clarinet
00292729 Alto Sax
00292730 Tenor Sax
00292732 Trumpet
00292733 Horn
00292735 Trombone
00292736 Violin
00292737 Viola
00292738 Cello

The Greatest Showman
8 songs
00277389 Flute
00277390 Clarinet
00277391 Alto Sax
00277392 Tenor Sax
00277393 Trumpet
00277394 Horn
00277395 Trombone
00277396 Violin
00277397 Viola
00277398 Cello

Irish Favorites
31 songs
00842489 Flute
00842490 Clarinet
00842491 Alto Sax
00842493 Trumpet
00842494 Horn
00842495 Trombone
00842496 Violin
00842497 Viola
00842498 Cello

Michael Jackson
11 songs
00119495 Flute
00119496 Clarinet
00119497 Alto Sax
00119498 Tenor Sax
00119499 Trumpet
00119501 Trombone
00119503 Violin
00119502 Accomp.

Jazz & Blues
14 songs
00841438 Flute
00841439 Clarinet
00841440 Alto Sax
00841442 Tenor Sax
00841441 Trumpet
00841443 Trombone
00841444 Violin

Jazz Classics
12 songs
00151812 Flute
00151813 Clarinet
00151814 Alto Sax
00151815 Tenor Sax
00151816 Trumpet
00151818 Trombone
00151819 Violin
00151821 Cello

Les Misérables
13 songs
00842292 Flute
00842293 Clarinet
00842294 Alto Sax
00842295 Tenor Sax
00842296 Trumpet
00842297 Horn
00842298 Trombone
00842299 Violin
00842300 Viola
00842301 Cello

Metallica
12 songs
02501327 Flute
02501339 Clarinet
02501332 Alto Sax
02501333 Tenor Sax
02501330 Trumpet
02502454 Horn
02501329 Trombone
02501334 Violin
02501335 Viola
02501338 Cello

Motown Classics
15 songs
00842572 Flute
00842573 Clarinet
00842574 Alto Sax
00842575 Tenor Sax
00842576 Trumpet
00842578 Trombone
00842579 Violin

Pirates of the Caribbean
16 songs
00842183 Flute
00842184 Clarinet
00842185 Alto Sax
00842186 Tenor Sax
00842187 Trumpet
00842188 Horn
00842189 Trombone
00842190 Violin
00842191 Viola
00842192 Cello

Queen
17 songs
00285402 Flute
00285403 Clarinet
00285404 Alto Sax
00285405 Tenor Sax
00285406 Trumpet
00285407 Horn
00285408 Trombone
00285409 Violin
00285410 Viola
00285411 Cello

Simple Songs
14 songs
00249081 Flute
00249093 Oboe
00249082 Clarinet
00249083 Alto Sax
00249084 Tenor Sax
00249086 Trumpet
00249087 Horn
00249089 Trombone
00249090 Violin
00249091 Viola
00249092 Cello
00249094 Mallets

Superhero Themes
14 songs
00363195 Flute
00363196 Clarinet
00363197 Alto Sax
00363198 Tenor Sax
00363199 Trumpet
00363200 Horn
00363201 Trombone
00363202 Violin
00363203 Viola
00363204 Cello

Star Wars
16 songs
00350900 Flute
00350913 Oboe
00350903 Clarinet
00350904 Alto Sax
00350905 Tenor Sax
00350906 Trumpet
00350907 Horn
00350908 Trombone
00350909 Violin
00350910 Viola
00350911 Cello
00350914 Mallet

Taylor Swift
15 songs
00842532 Flute
00842533 Clarinet
00842534 Alto Sax
00842535 Tenor Sax
00842536 Trumpet
00842537 Horn
00842538 Trombone
00842539 Violin
00842540 Viola
00842541 Cello

Video Game Music
13 songs
00283877 Flute
00283878 Clarinet
00283879 Alto Sax
00283880 Tenor Sax
00283882 Trumpet
00283883 Horn
00283884 Trombone
00283885 Violin
00283886 Viola
00283887 Cello

Wicked
13 songs
00842236 Flute
00842237 Clarinet
00842238 Alto Sax
00842239 Tenor Sax
00842240 Trumpet
00842241 Horn
00842242 Trombone
00842243 Violin
00842244 Viola
00842245 Cello

HAL•LEONARD®

0122
488

HAL•LEONARD

Classical PLAY-ALONG™

The Hal Leonard Classical Play-Along™ series will help you play great classical pieces. Listen to the full performance tracks to hear how the piece sounds with an orchestra, and then play along using the accompaniment tracks. The audio CD is playable on any CD player. For PC and Mac computer users, the CD is enhanced so you can adjust the recording to any tempo without changing pitch.

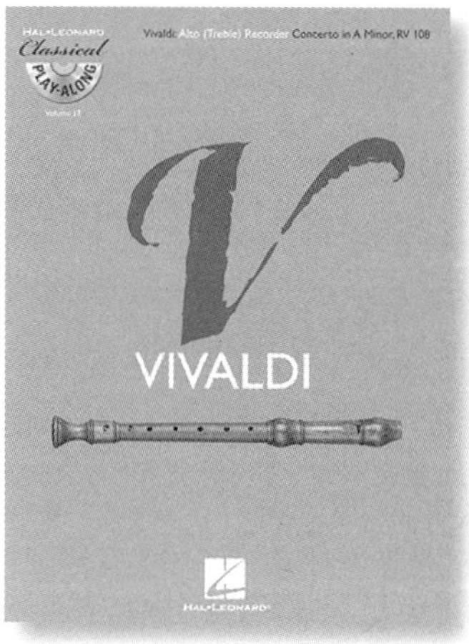

1. MOZART:
FLUTE CONCERTO IN D MAJOR, K314
Book/CD Pack
00842341 Flute........$12.99

2. SAMMARTINI:
DESCANT (SOPRANO) RECORDER CONCERTO IN F MAJOR
Book/CD Pack
00842342 Soprano Recorder........$12.99

3. LOEILLET:
TREBLE (ALTO) RECORDER SONATA IN G MAJOR, OP.1, NO.3
Book/CD Pack
00842343 Alto Recorder........$12.99

4. MOZART:
CLARINET CONCERTO IN A MAJOR, K622
Book/CD Pack
00842344 Clarinet........$12.99

6. MOZART:
HORN CONCERTO IN D MAJOR, K412/514
Book/CD Pack
00842346 Horn........$12.99

7. BACH:
VIOLIN CONCERTO IN A MINOR, BWV 1041
Book/CD Pack
00842347 Violin........$12.99

8. TELEMANN:
VIOLA CONCERTO IN G MAJOR, TWV 51:G9
Book/Online Audio
00842348 Viola........$12.99

9. HAYDN:
CELLO CONCERTO IN C MAJOR, HOB. VIIB: 1
Book/CD Pack
00842349 Cello........$12.99

10. BACH:
PIANO CONCERTO IN F MINOR, BWV 1056
Book/CD Pack
00842350 Piano........$12.99

11. PERGOLESI:
FLUTE CONCERTO IN G MAJOR
Book/CD Pack
00842351 Flute........$12.99

12. BARRE:
DESCANT (SOPRANO) RECORDER SUITE NO. 9 "DEUXIEME LIVRE" G MAJOR
Book/Online Audio
00842352 Soprano Recorder........$12.99

14. VON WEBER:
CLARINET CONCERTO NO. 1 IN F MINOR, OP. 73
Book/CD Pack
00842354 Clarinet........$12.99

15. MOZART:
VIOLIN CONCERTO IN G MAJOR, K216
Book/CD Pack
00842355 Violin........$12.99

16. BOCCHERINI:
CELLO CONCERTO IN B-FLAT MAJOR, G482
Book/CD Pack
00842356 Cello........$12.99

17. MOZART:
PIANO CONCERTO IN C MAJOR, K467
Book/CD Pack
00842357 Piano........$12.99

18. BACH:
FLUTE SONATA IN E-FLAT MAJOR, BWV 1031
Book/CD Pack
00842450 Flute........$12.99

19. BRAHMS:
CLARINET SONATA IN F MINOR, OP. 120, NO. 1
Book/CD Pack
00842451 Clarinet........$12.99

20. BEETHOVEN:
TWO ROMANCES FOR VIOLIN, OP. 40 IN G & OP. 50 IN F
Book/CD Pack
00842452 Violin........$12.99

21. MOZART:
PIANO CONCERTO IN D MINOR, K466
Book/CD Pack
00842453 Piano........$12.99